ALTERNATOR
BOOKS™

THE
CIVIL
RIGHTS
MOVEMENT

ERIC BRAUN

Lerner Publications ◆ Minneapolis

Lerner Publications Company
A division of Lerner Publishing Group, Inc.
241 First Avenue North
Minneapolis, MN 55401 USA

For reading levels and more information, look up this title at www.lernerbooks.com.

Main body text set in Aptifer Slab LT Pro Regular 11.5/18.
Typeface provided by Linotype AG.

Library of Congress Cataloging-in-Publication Data

Names: Braun, Eric, 1971– author.
Title: The Civil Rights Movement / Eric Braun.
Description: Minneapolis : Lerner Publications, 2019. | Includes
    bibliographical references and index.
Identifiers: LCCN 2017053570 (print) | LCCN 2017047867 (ebook) |
    ISBN 9781541525566 (eb pdf) | ISBN 9781541523319 (lb : alk. paper)
Subjects: LCSH: African Americans—Civil rights—History—20th
    century—Juvenile literature. | Civil rights movements—United
    States—History—20th century—Juvenile literature. | United
    States—Race relations—Juvenile literature.
Classification: LCC E185.61 (print) | LCC E185.61 .B7918 2019 (ebook) |
    DDC 323.1196/0730904—dc23

LC record available at https://lccn.loc.gov/2017053570

Manufactured in the United States of America
1-44404-34663-2/26/2018

CONTENTS

MARCH ON WASHINGTON

It's August 28, 1963. The National Mall in Washington, DC, is filling with people. They've come from across the country in buses, trains, planes, and cars. They plan to march in support of **civil rights** for black Americans.

The crowd begins to march to the Lincoln Memorial. They carry signs calling for voting rights and ending **segregated** rules in public schools. Organizers of this March

Protesters fill the National Mall at the 1963 March on Washington for Jobs and Freedom.

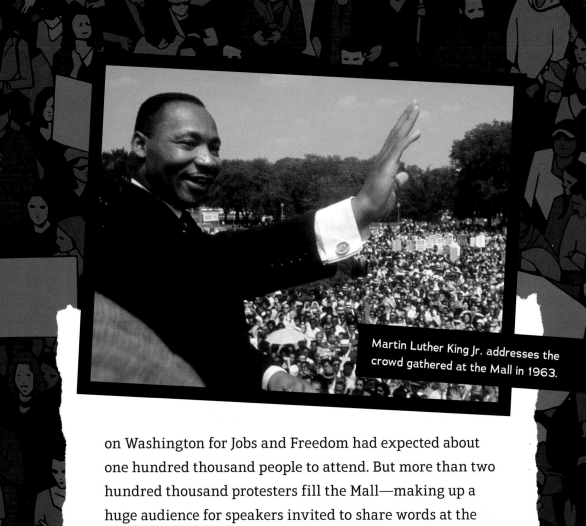

Martin Luther King Jr. addresses the crowd gathered at the Mall in 1963.

on Washington for Jobs and Freedom had expected about one hundred thousand people to attend. But more than two hundred thousand protesters fill the Mall—making up a huge audience for speakers invited to share words at the event.

The final speaker of the day is Martin Luther King Jr. He speaks of his dream that one day the United States will no longer treat people of different races differently. The speech becomes known as the "I Have a Dream" speech—and it goes down in history as one of the civil rights movement's defining moments.

CHAPTER 1

BIRTH OF A MOVEMENT

The civil rights movement peaked in the 1960s. But its roots stretch back to the end of the Civil War (1861–1865). Following the war, three **amendments** to the US Constitution granted rights to African Americans. The Thirteenth Amendment ended slavery in 1865. Three years later, the Fourteenth Amendment granted citizenship to former slaves. And in 1870, the Fifteenth Amendment gave black American men the right to vote.

This painting depicts the Battle of Gettysburg, a major confrontation in the Civil War.

But many white people resisted these changes. They created laws making it hard for black people to vote. Some laws made people pay fees and take reading tests before they could vote. Few black citizens had the money to pay the fees or the reading ability to pass the tests.

Other laws made it legal to segregate black people from white people. These laws said black people could be denied access to schools, parks, and other public places if they were offered a separate but equal option. But whites determined what separate but equal meant. And it was very rarely equal.

Drinking fountains were often segregated, as was this fountain near the Halifax County Courthouse in North Carolina.

A Moment in the Movement

In December 1955, a black woman named Rosa Parks (*below*) caught a segregated bus in Montgomery, Alabama. She took a seat in a section for black passengers. The bus began to fill with white passengers. When the section for white passengers was full, the driver told Parks to give up her seat. She refused. The driver called the police, who arrested Parks.

Parks's refusal to give up her seat sparked a **boycott** of Montgomery buses by black riders. Another important leader of the boycott was a young civil rights **activist** named Martin Luther King Jr. The effort that he and Parks put into the boycott led to a US Supreme Court ruling that Montgomery **integrate** its buses—and it also led to King's and Parks's emergence as leaders of the civil rights movement.

A NEW ORGANIZATION

In the late nineteenth century and early twentieth century, African Americans had few options to protest their treatment. One of the first organized attempts to fight **discrimination** in the United States was the National Association for the Advancement of Colored People (NAACP). Activists started this organization in 1909. They fought for black rights in court and in public opinion. But discriminatory laws continued.

Four of the most active leaders of the NAACP were (*left to right*) Henry L. Moon, Roy Wilkins, Herbert Hill, and Thurgood Marshall.

BROWN V. BOARD OF EDUCATION

Then, in 1954, the US Supreme Court ruled in *Brown v. Board of Education* that it was illegal to segregate black and white students. The government told public schools to integrate, but many whites resisted. In 1957, for example, the Little Rock, Arkansas, school board ordered Central High School to integrate. Nine African American students signed up for classes. But the Arkansas governor ordered the National Guard to block the students. A few weeks later, President Dwight D. Eisenhower ordered the governor to allow the students to enter the school.

The African American students who signed up for classes at Central High enter the building escorted by soldiers.

That same year, President Eisenhower signed the Civil Rights Act of 1957. The bill didn't offer African Americans any new rights, but it protected black Americans' right to vote. Critics felt the new law was too weak to be important—but it was the first major civil rights law passed by Congress in eighty-two years.

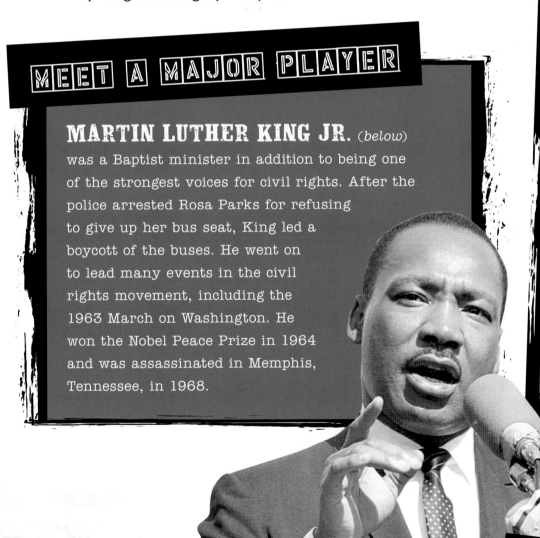

MEET A MAJOR PLAYER

MARTIN LUTHER KING JR. *(below)* was a Baptist minister in addition to being one of the strongest voices for civil rights. After the police arrested Rosa Parks for refusing to give up her bus seat, King led a boycott of the buses. He went on to lead many events in the civil rights movement, including the 1963 March on Washington. He won the Nobel Peace Prize in 1964 and was assassinated in Memphis, Tennessee, in 1968.

CHAPTER 2

THE MOVEMENT BUILDS

The 1960s marked some of the country's most notable activism on behalf of civil rights. The decade also included groundbreaking laws and legal victories for the movement. One of the first monumental events of the 1960s was the Greensboro **sit-in**.

archers carrying US flags and
hers protest a racially motivated
ch bombing in Alabama in 1963.

Young people in Greensboro, North Carolina, fill seats at Woolworth's lunch counter to protest the establishment's refusal to serve them.

On February 1, 1960, four black college students sat at the Woolworth's lunch counter in Greensboro, North Carolina. The counter served only white customers. When the staff denied service to the black students, they refused to give up their seats. The police were called, but they didn't know how to react to this new type of protest. When the lunch counter closed that night, the students left. But they returned the next day with more students. Within days, protesters filled every seat. The media picked up the story. The news inspired similar protests elsewhere.

FREEDOM RIDES

Civil rights activists tried other forms of protest too. In 1961 activists planned bus trips called Freedom Rides. Freedom Riders boarded buses in southern cities. At each stop, black riders tried to use restrooms and other facilities labeled "whites only."

Early in their trip, the group received little notice. But soon white protesters began meeting the riders at their stops and attacking them. On May 14, protesters threw a bomb into a bus. The Freedom Rides continued throughout the summer. Finally, in September, the federal government called for integrating interstate transportation such as buses.

Freedom Riders whose bus was set on fire by white counterprotesters look on as smoke billows from the vehicle.

MEET A MAJOR PLAYER

FANNIE LOU HAMER helped organize the 1964 Freedom Summer African American voter registration drive in Mississippi. Much of her activism focused on getting black Americans registered to vote. But she was also known for singing songs such as "Go Tell It on the Mountain" to keep activists inspired. Hamer was part of the Mississippi Freedom Democratic Party, a group of activists who in 1964 questioned the legality of Mississippi's segregated, all-white delegation.

AN ONGOING FIGHT

In spite of progress made by the sit-ins and Freedom Rides, discriminatory laws continued. And activists continued to use protests to change things. In 1963 the March on Washington was televised. Many felt the media attention helped bring about the Civil Rights Act of 1964, which expanded on the 1957 act. One year later, the media covered protesters at the Selma-to-Montgomery March. Eight days after that, President Lyndon B. Johnson urged Congress to support the Voting Rights Act. It became law in 1965.

A Moment in the Movement

On March 7, 1965, protesters began marching from Selma, Alabama, to the state capitol in Montgomery to promote civil rights (*pictured below*). But they weren't marching long before police attacked them. Protesters tried the march again two days later, but this time, they turned back, fearing a second confrontation.

Johnson pledged his support for the protesters, and a US district court judge ordered the governor of Alabama to allow the march. Federal troops were called in to protect the marchers. They set out again on March 21, and they marched for hours each day, stopping only to sleep in fields. They finally arrived in Montgomery on March 25.

BLACK POWER AND THE BLACK PANTHERS

Not everyone agreed with nonviolent protest methods. Activists Malcolm X and Stokely Carmichael promoted the idea of black power. They believed black citizens needed to defend themselves against white violence by using violence themselves. And in 1966, Huey P. Newton and Bobby Seale formed the Black Panther Party. It demanded rights for black Americans, including an end to police brutality. It supported the use of force against police when necessary.

The Panthers and the black power movement were only a small part of the 1960s civil rights movement. Many others followed King's nonviolent approach. All the activists were fighting for civil rights. They just disagreed on how to go about it.

Malcolm X spoke at many protests and rallies to advance the black power cause.

CHAPTER 3

THE ROAD TO BLACK LIVES MATTER

The civil rights movement didn't end with the 1960s. Activists didn't consider their work done. Black families often continued to live in less desirable parts of cities or towns. They often had less access to health care and opportunities for employment. In 1970 black men were earning on average about 60 percent of what white men earned.

Low-wage jobs were often the only jobs available for African Americans in the 1960s and 1970s.

Protesters in the women's rights movement, such as these women taking to the streets in 1970, were emboldened by the progress made by civil rights activists.

Yet there was proof of the success of the civil rights movement: By the 1970s, other movements were copying the methods of civil rights protesters. The women's rights movement, the environmental rights movement, and the gay rights movement all drew on the success of the civil rights movement. For the next few decades, civil rights activists often worked with activists from other movements to achieve change.

ROCKED BY VIOLENCE

By the 2010s, however, a series of events led to a renewed sense of urgency for achieving civil rights for black Americans. One such event occurred in Florida in February 2012. A black teenager named Trayvon Martin was walking home from a store when George Zimmerman, a neighborhood resident of white and Hispanic descent, shot and killed him. Though Zimmerman was charged with murder, he claimed Martin had attacked him, and he was **acquitted**.

Protesters in Sanford, Florida, call for justice after Trayvon Martin was killed.

The #BlackLivesMatter movement spread from social media to the streets as concern about violence against African Americans grew.

Media covered the event. Some white people blamed Martin for his own death instead of Zimmerman for killing him. A group of activists started the #BlackLivesMatter hashtag on social media. They said that antiblack racism was still a powerful force in the United States.

The parents of Michael Brown, who was fatally shot by a police officer, appear at a protest against racially motivated violence by police.

Two years later, another unarmed black teen was killed, this time by a police officer. Michael Brown was shot in Ferguson, Missouri. Again, the media covered the event. And again, many people were angered to hear people blaming Brown instead of the officer who shot him.

A protest broke out in Ferguson. The police responded with tanks, tear gas, and rubber bullets. The protest escalated, and over the following days, police arrested 172 people. The scene in Ferguson was a breaking point for many black citizens who felt oppressed by the police. They felt the country didn't care about what happened to black people.

FROM HASHTAG TO
SOCIAL MOVEMENT

In the next few years, more African Americans were killed or attacked. Witnesses captured several of these events on cell phone cameras and shared them on social media. People who hadn't considered themselves activists soon became supporters of the #BlackLivesMatter movement.

Students who support #BlackLivesMatter come together for a march from Martin Luther King Jr. Park in Minneapolis, Minnesota.

More than ever, average citizens were becoming vocal activists for civil rights. Celebrities also began speaking out. In 2016 San Francisco 49ers quarterback Colin Kaepernick began sitting and later kneeling instead of standing as the national anthem played before games. He was protesting the killing of minorities by police. Soon other NFL players were joining him.

CHAPTER 4

THE FUTURE

Protest continues to be a powerful tool in the civil rights movement. In August 2017, civil rights activists gathered when **white supremacists** held a rally in Charlottesville, Virginia. The activists carried signs reading, "Black Lives Matter" and "Love."

A woman protests the August 2017 rally by white supremacists in Charlottesville.

Clashes broke out between the white supremacists and the civil rights activists. The August weekend turned especially violent when a white supremacist intentionally drove his car into a crowd of anti-racists, killing one and injuring about thirty others. The act of violence shocked many Americans. It left the country—as well as many around the world—feeling sad.

KEEP ON FIGHTING

Many Americans were deeply distressed to realize that racism is still so prevalent in the United States. Yet the anti-racist message spread by the activists heartened lots of people. It encouraged some who hadn't previously been involved in civil rights causes to add their voices to the movement. For others, it was encouragement to keep on fighting.

Every day, ordinary people continue to protest for civil rights in small and big ways. African Americans and their allies will never give up in the ongoing fight for equality.

Protesters make their voices heard at the March for Racial Justice in Washington, DC, on September 30, 2017.

Timeline

1865–1870: The Thirteenth through Fifteenth Amendments grant critical rights to African Americans, including ending slavery, granting citizenship, and giving African American men the right to vote.

1909: The National Association for the Advancement of Colored People (NAACP) is founded.

1954: The Supreme Court rules in *Brown v. Board of Education* that it is illegal to segregate black and white students in public schools.

1955: Rosa Parks sparks a bus boycott in Montgomery, Alabama, when she refuses to give up her seat to a white rider.

1957: Central High School in Little Rock, Arkansas, is integrated. President Eisenhower signs the Civil Rights Act of 1957.

1960: Four black college students stage the Greensboro sit-in.

1961: The Freedom Rides spark violence across southern states when black riders attempt to use whites-only facilities at bus stations.

1963: More than two hundred thousand marchers attend the March on Washington for Jobs and Freedom.

1964: President Johnson signs the Civil Rights Act of 1964, greatly expanding the 1957 act.

1965: The Selma-to-Montgomery March takes place. President Johnson signs the Voting Rights Act.

1966: The Black Panther Party forms.

2012: George Zimmerman shoots Trayvon Martin in Florida.

2013: The #BlackLivesMatter movement is founded.

2014: A police officer shoots Michael Brown in Ferguson, Missouri.

2016: NFL quarterback Colin Kaepernick takes a knee during the national anthem.

2017: A white supremacist rally in Charlottesville, Virginia, leads to one death and many injuries among counterprotesters.

Glossary

acquitted: declared not guilty of a crime in a court of law

activist: a person who actively supports or opposes one side of an issue

amendments: changes or additions to a document, such as the US Constitution. Amendments to the constitution change the basic laws of the country.

boycott: to refuse to use, buy, or participate in something as a form of protest

civil rights: the rights of a citizen

discrimination: treating people differently, usually in a negative way, based on their race, religion, gender, or other differences

integrate: to bring together to give members of different groups equal opportunities

segregated: set apart from others, especially as a means of discrimination against one race

sit-in: a protest in which people stay in a place and refuse to leave until their demands are met

white supremacists: people who believe that white people are better than people of color

Further Information

Adamson, Thomas K. *The Civil War.* New York: Smartbook Media, 2017.

Aretha, David. *The Story of the Selma Voting Rights Marches in Photographs.* Berkeley Heights, NJ: Enslow, 2014.

Braun, Eric. *Taking Action for Civil and Political Rights.* Minneapolis: Lerner Publications, 2017.

Hooks, Gwendolyn. *If You Were a Kid during the Civil Rights Movement.* New York: Children's Press, 2017.

Millender, Dharathula H. *Martin Luther King, Jr.* New York: Aladdin, 2014.

National Civil Rights Museum
https://www.civilrightsmuseum.org

Seattle Times—Martin Luther King Jr.: An Extraordinary Life
http://projects.seattletimes.com/mlk/?utm_source=redirect&utm_medium=vanityURL&utm_campaign=redirect

Winter, Max. *The Civil Rights Movement.* North Mankato, MN: Abdo, 2014.

Index

Photo Acknowledgments

The images in this book are used with the permission of: Robert W. Kelley/The LIFE Picture Collection/Getty Images, p. 4; Francis Miller/The LIFE Picture Collection/Getty Images, p. 5; Wikipedia Commons/Kurz and Allison/Mmxx (PD), p. 6; Library of Congress, pp. 7, 9, 18; Don Cravens/The LIFE Images Collection/Getty Images, p. 8; National Archives, p. 10; Michael Ochs Archives/Getty Images, p. 11; Chicago History Museum/Getty Images, p. 12; Bettmann/Getty Images, pp. 13, 16; Underwood Archives/Archive Photos/Getty Images, p. 14; Bob Parent/Hulton Archive/Getty Images, p. 17; Don Carl Steffen/Gamma-Rapho/Getty Images, p. 19; Ira Bostic/Shutterstock.com, p. 20; The All-Nite Images/Wikimedia Commons (CC by-SA 2.0), p. 21; Aaron P. Bernstein/Stringer/Getty Images, p. 22; Fibonacci Blue/Flickr (CC by 2.0), p. 23; Michael Zagaris/Getty Images, p. 24; Chip Somodevilla/Getty Images, pp. 25, 26. Design elements: Kair/Shutterstock.com; rob zs/Shutterstock.com; Miloje/Shutterstock.com; rob zs/Shutterstock.com; Milan M/Shutterstock.com.

Cover: Don Cravens/The LIFE Images Collection/Getty Images (Rosa Parks); Al Diaz/Miami Herald/TNS/Getty Images (Colin Kaepernick); a katz/Shutterstock.com (Black Lives Matter); Library of Congress (Dr. Martin Luther King, Jr. and March on Washington).